next chapter

Kayla Blake

BookLeaf Publishing

Presentation by *BookLeaf Publishing*

Web: www.bookleafpub.com

E-mail: info@bookleafpub.com

ISBN : 9789357699525

First edition 2022

DEDICATION

This book is dedicated to my dearest friend, Gabriella Aabott.

ACKNOWLEDGEMENT

I'd first like to thank God for the opportunity that he gave me in publish these poems. Second id like to thank my family for their support of me and my writing efforts over the years. And lastly, any friends that have stuck by me through this process. Without all of you there along side me i would not have been able to do this.

PREFACE

Dear Reader,
Hi my name is Kayla. I am a Christian artist and small town writer. I have been using my writing talents to bring life and joy into the lives of those closest to me. Now i've decided to try to share my voice with those that buy this book. I chose the title of this book Next Chapter because i thought it was fitting for the many poems written inside here.

To me Next Chapter means that you have more to your story. That life can go on and most of these poems were crafted during some of my most difficult seasons. I found a lot of comfort in them over the years as i wrote them. I hope that you might be able to gain something from them that will help you along your own road in life too.

You Understand

You understand why I'm clumsy
You understand why I fail and need your
encouragement
You understand why I'm different and stay out of
the crowd
You understand why I write with a passion
You understand why I am who I am
That's most important because now you
understand me

Have you ever noticed the stars?

Have you ever noticed the stars?
How the shine so big and bright
Way up in the sky they are
They hide until night fall
Then they forget to be shy
and shine with all their might and glory
Have you ever noticed the stars?
They shine so peacefully and quietly
It is amazing how they twinkle

Imagine

There is a thing that all of us have
Some use it often and others think they can't
If you look deep inside of yourself
There you will find what always has been there
Behind the mind
In the mind
A memory
A dream
Or a simple thought is always imagined here
Inside a child and even adult
Lies the very heart of all things thought

Heart or Mind

My mind has been stuck on you for a while now
For months to be exact
I feel like i love you
but i cant seem to untangle my mind
I think its all in my head but my heart tells me otherwise
My mind is as loud as my heart
thats why i tell myself
No
I don't love you
I feel like I'm too young to know what love is
I always follow my heart but this time my mind is in the way
It sends me spiraling thoughts that it will never work
I think relationships don't last
I feel like i could make it work but I'm also afraid
My confidence wavers and i think i will break your
heart again
I need to find answers because i know you still love me

Do you still love me?

You still love me
I know its true
I can tell it in your voice when you speak to me
It hides in your laugh when i say something
funny
I can see it in your face behind your smile
I can see it in your as they shine deeply
Your heart is big and pure
But theres always room for me
You still love me
I know its true

If only

If only i could see you staring at me
If only i could feel you express your love for me
If only i could hear your laugh of joy
If only i could see your eyes and lose myself in them
If only i could see you smiling at me
If only
If only I had a wish
I'd wish you were here with me so that i could see you

The Moon

Big and beautiful
It sits quietly in the dark
It shines bright
It comes in different shapes
It decides when it should show its true beauty
It decides when to hide
If you sit quietly
alone in the dark
It will come and shine in all its might

In Between

In the dark there is nothingness
In the light there is growing
In the shadows there is emptiness
In the glow there is a shine
In doubt there is hoping
In the waiting there is patience
In weakness there is strength
In the defeated there is yet fight
In failure there is grace
.

I love you

I love you
I know i do
It took me a while
but im glad i found you
I know i love you
I can feel it bubbling up inside me
Its weakening and i stumble
but your loving hand catches me
I love you
Yes, I do
But do you still feel it, too?

Shine Bright

Hello little star
There you are
I see you
Don't be shy
Come out to play
Without you the night is dull
You make all the others beautiful
So don't be shy
Come out and shine
Shine with all your glory

Expressing

A picture can express a thousand words
Words can express a million emotions
But silence is different
It can speak much
Or it can be deafening
More can happen in a single moment of silence
than what could happen in a thousand years

Big Blue Sky

Big blue sky
way up high
As far as the eye can see
like an endless ocean
a blanket over the earth
soft gentle clouds
shaping a picture to ponder
you can sit for hours looking at its beauty
time flies when your looking into the big blue
sky

Life’s what you make it

Life is what you make it
Don't throw it away
It goes by so fast
It'll be gone before you know it
So don't waste it
Make the most of it
While you still can
Go for it
Take the risk
Accept the opportunity
Use it
Don't abuse it
Because you might lose it
So make the most of it

It is well

You fill me with life
You save me from death
I was dead
But now i live
because of your sustaining love
I am not worthy
But i am chosen despite it
Truly, I say it is well with my soul

Thoughts

Quietly thinking
Waiting
Silence comes
quiet still
Whispers of the past
Fade away
Hope of the future
Come to stay
Moment happens
Right here today
They fade
They are created new

Moment of Youth

I found your picture today
It was wrinkled and torn
I unfolded it and straightened it
Instantly memories came flooding back to me
One after the other
Like a never ending flood
I smiled softly to myself as i enjoyed those forgotten memories
I cherished them for one last time
Then i gently slipped it back into the cardboard box
To forget them once again

Life’s Road

Life's road is long
It winds and curves
Sometimes it goes up
Other times it goes down
It has bumps and cracks you can easily fall into
But there's always a lesson
Or an experience earned
It gets tough
People get hurt
But in the end you always
Find some way to get back up
And keep traveling life's long road

Created to be

I am created to be loved
I am created to be known
I am fearfully and wonderfully made
I'm carefully woven together
I'm made new
All of the pieces of me
Reflect all of the pieces of you
I am created to be enough
I am created to be me

Breathe

Breathe in
Take a moment
Settle in
Clear your mind
Focus
Breathe out
Push the thought away
Forget the task on hand
Don't worry over that thing
Breathe in
Fill your lungs with air
Your mind with a positive thought
Connect with your heart
Breathe out
Feel the weight lift
Let go of control
Believe the truth and let go of the lie
Breathe in
Peace of mind
Calmness of heart
Rest in the clarity of the moment
Breathe out
Take a step
Know the answer
Walk in the knowing

As I sit quietly

As i sit quietly
I can sense you there
In the stillness of twilight
I can find you in the morning sun
Resting in the dew drops of fallen rain
In the color of autumn leaves
And the warmth of a smile
Like a friend i've always known
Never far
Always nearer still
In the quiet night
And the soft glow of the stars
In the wonder of a child
And breath of new life
As i sit quietly I know where i can find you

Am I Worthy?

Am I worthy?
Who is a worthy soul?
Is there one person to be found chosen as
righteous?
I tell you there is not one
Are we doomed to forever walk in the dark?
Where do we go to be made new?
The waters of the Earth can not cleanse us
We are dirty, rotten and dead
Where can we find new life?
Among ourselves there is nothing
The beasts of the Earth devour us
In the night we are torn apart
Yet, in the dark I find your light
It leads me to search for you
I find you in the light
Way up on a hill
Your rest is my comfort
Your truth is everlasting

www.ingramcontent.com/pod-product-compliance
Lightning Source LLC
Chambersburg PA
CBHW062110140826
49812CB00058B/1215